(

St Pat

KEVIN SAMBROOK

St Patrick's Breastplate

I arise today
Through a mighty strength, the invocation of the
Trinity,
Through belief in the Threeness,
Through confession of the Oneness
of the Creator of creation.

I arise today
Through the strength of Christ's birth with His
baptism,
Through the strength of His crucifixion with His burial,
Through the strength of His resurrection with His
ascension,
Through the strength of His descent for the judgment
of doom.

I arise today
Through the strength of the love of cherubim,
In the obedience of angels,
In the service of archangels,
In the hope of resurrection to meet with reward,
In the prayers of patriarchs,
In the predictions of prophets,
In the preaching of apostles,
In the faith of confessors,
In the innocence of holy virgins,
In the deeds of righteous men.

I arise today, through
The strength of heaven,
The light of the sun,

The radiance of the moon,
The splendour of fire,
The speed of lightning,
The swiftness of wind,
The depth of the sea,
The stability of the earth,
The firmness of rock.

I arise today, through
God's strength to pilot me,
God's might to uphold me,
God's wisdom to guide me,
God's eye to look before me,
God's ear to hear me,
God's word to speak for me,
God's hand to guard me,
God's shield to protect me,
God's host to save me
From snares of devils,
From temptation of vices,
From everyone who shall wish me ill,
afar and near.

I summon today
All these powers between me and those evils,
Against every cruel and merciless power
that may oppose my body and soul,
Against incantations of false prophets,
Against black laws of pagandom,
Against false laws of heretics,
Against craft of idolatry,
Against spells of witches and smiths and wizards,
Against every knowledge that corrupts man's body
and soul;

Christ to shield me today
Against poison, against burning,
Against drowning, against wounding,
So that there may come to me an abundance of
reward.

Christ with me,
Christ before me,
Christ behind me,
Christ in me,
Christ beneath me,
Christ above me,
Christ on my right,
Christ on my left,
Christ when I lie down,
Christ when I sit down,
Christ when I arise,
Christ in the heart of every man who thinks of me,
Christ in the mouth of everyone who speaks of me,
Christ in every eye that sees me,
Christ in every ear that hears me.

I arise today
Through a mighty strength, the invocation of the
Trinity,
Through belief in the Threeness,
Through confession of the Oneness
of the Creator of creation.

Foreword

Ireland is a land of countless portal tombs thought to be final resting places for saints and scholars and legendary warriors, poets, and kings. Its history is steeped in legends and stories wrapped in truth and uncertainties. Radiant green hills and ocean cliffs are dotted with bee-hive huts and Celtic crosses that stand as stoic reminders of its intriguing past. No one has stood center stage and dominated Ireland's historic past like Patrick. He has played the contradictory leading role in the fables and folklore and no one has been cloaked in more fallacies than he. Not only is he the greatest and most dominant of Ireland's three patron saints, he is also the most celebrated Irish Catholic in history, yet he was never Irish or Catholic. A character of incredible contradiction, he challenged the dark idolatry on the land and lighted the hills with fiery truth. He operated in signs and wonders and performed miracles that rivaled Old Testament heroes. He not only introduced Ireland to the power of the God of heaven, he also introduced Ireland to the love of the God of heaven. I believe that his sacrificial obedience and the pure love of God that he demonstrated to his despisers in his generation is the reason he is known today. Which proves once again that love is stronger than death.

Kevin has captured the story of this amazing man in a powerful, inspiring, and refreshingly concise read. Void of fable and folklore, this book truly cuts straight to the heart of Patrick's mission and message. A must read for those who are "chosen" for kingdom adventures in our generation. You will be amazed by his story as you grasp what can be accomplished through love and obedience, and the impact and influence that follows in its wake.

Ray Hughes

Selah Ministries

Acknowledgements

I am indebted to my precious wife Rose for her encouragement and for applying the necessary pressure to me to get this book written. Special thanks to Stephen Bond, Fiona Rutherford, Kim Balding and Michael Harper for casting their expert eyes over the text and helping with editing. Thanks also to James Nesbit for doing the Graphic Design Cover and to Ian Moffat for the beautiful photo of Mount Slemish. I am grateful to my dear family members including my parents Jim and Felicity, Rose's mum Sheila and Melanie for their love and support in this project. And not forgetting my own precious Church family at Covenant Love and the many other dear friends too, without whom this would not have been possible.

Kevin Sambrook

KEVIN SAMBROOK

INTRODUCTION

I have long been fascinated with St Patrick's story. Much of his life is unknown. Myths and legends have grown around this enigmatic man, some exaggerated others untrue. The little we do know about him comes to us through his own writings, namely his *Confession* and his *Letter to Coroticus*. These are held by secular historians to be authentic works of Patrick. His *Confession* is a response to slanderous accusations made against him by some jealous peers and includes significant details about his life work and ministry. Although it is an incomplete autobiography, it does furnish us with sufficient information to draw conclusions as to what Patrick was like, how he thought, how he saw his life's mission, and his reasons for continuing it until his death. It is from his *Confession* that I have sought to bring insights into the mind and character of the man. To draw from his life lessons and encouragement for us today. To make him accessible and within our reach.

Playing rugby three times a week plus training is what I was doing when I was sixteen. No cares, no responsibilities, selfish and self centred. A child growing into a man doing the usual things that teenage boys do. Of course 'teenager' is a recent term invented during the post war period for marketing purposes. Before

World War Two they didn't really exist. Photographs from the period show sons, fathers and grandfathers all dressed the same and working from an early age. Life was harder and the pleasures were simple. Few of the privileges that children take for granted today existed then. The past, they say, is another country.

One way to visit that foreign soil is through film. Cinema has created a visuality that fuels the imagination and moves the emotions. What it can't do, however, is enable you to live the drama. One can 'relive' something by watching a scene that reminds us of a past experience, but cinema – as good as it is – cannot place you in the danger it shows. You are not dodging bullets nor are you being chased or suffering the poverty and injustice in the story. You are simply an observer.

The difficulty when writing about the past is trying to describe what was going on inside the person, the hero, commanding the stage of history at that time. Facts can be sparse, leaving gaping holes. Missing pieces leave the jigsaw picture incomplete. These have to be 'found' somehow, by the storyteller. One solution is to try to place yourself 'there', in their shoes; to ask, how would I think, feel or respond if I were placed in the moment of high drama, excitement or danger present at that time as it happened?

This is what I have tried to do with the life of Patrick. I have not set out to write an exhaustive biography, but rather provide glimpses into his inner world at pivotal moments of his life. I am fascinated by the choices he made at those intersections in his life when he could have gone in any direction. His choices became hinges of history that have impacted countless lives, even nations. The effect has been immeasurable. The world was changed by them, yet Patrick would not have grasped that at the time. He simply wanted to do the right thing in the sight of God. He had no idea that he was to become the Patron Saint of Ireland or that his memory would be revered around the world. He lived one day at a time, surviving in brutal obscurity and learning to trust God as a slave in a foreign land. Most remarkable is the fact of how young he was when he started to 'choose.' He was just sixteen years old.

We inhabit an age of celebrity and fame gone mad, with its grotesque addiction to the limelight. By contrast Patrick's story is like breathing in the pure air of a mountain breeze. We feel the breath of God blow upon us through his life, still fresh and without a trace of staleness after one and a half millennia. This simple, uncomplicated man has left us a living legacy threaded with the grace of God.

His life was anything but easy. Not for him the warm study rooms of a theological seminary, but rather the hard earthy school of life in its most brutal form, slavery. It was during his six years of harsh servitude that the boy became a man, when he found God and was fashioned as God's instrument upon the anvil of adversity. Towering above all else in Patrick's story was his ability, with God's help, to make the right choice when it mattered. Patrick's shadow is long and ageless. It falls rather like Peter's shadow did as it healed the sick in the book of Acts. It is already cast beyond today, ready to touch the unborn lives of tomorrow, not in any mystical sense, but in the example of hope. The brave example of one so young, who cut a path for us to follow through the thick undergrowth of this world's pitfalls and pain.

Moses once told Israel, "I call heaven and earth to record this day against you, that I have set before you life and death, blessing and cursing: therefore choose life that thou and thy seed may live." (Deuteronomy 30:19 KJV). Whilst many traumatic events robbed him of innocence, we see Patrick consistently choosing to look Godward, choosing life and blessing. Seldom do we see in any man the ability to trust God so wholeheartedly in what some would describe as 'a cruel twist of fate'.

It would have been tempting to accept the counsel of Job's wife to "curse God and die!" but Patrick refused to do that. His resilience and ability to walk the narrow path of destiny owed everything to God's redemptive power, God working "all things after the counsel of His own will."

Yet we must not allow that to diminish Patrick's part. Although he did not rise to become a powerful civic leader, his life parallels that of Joseph in Egypt. We can trace the same journey from kidnap, slavery, and deliverance, followed by the eventual rise to a place of prominence, exerting a huge influence upon a great mass of people. In each case, it is the power of choices that almost blinds the eye and sparkles upon our consciousness, like pure sunlight reflected from the surface of a precious jewel. Without making these critical choices, both Joseph and Patrick would have sunk into blackness and oblivion. Just two more victims of man's inhumanity lost in a sea of forgotten slaves. Without those choices the world around them would not have changed the way it did and entire regions would have remained in darkness.

Patrick is thought to have passed from this world, physically on 17th March AD 461. In another sense, however, he has never left, for, 'God [is] testifying of his gifts: and by it he being dead yet speaketh.' (Hebrews 11:4 KJV)

CHAPTER ONE

BACKGROUND[1]

Patrick was born to proud parents Calpurnius and Concessa into the privileged ruling class of Roman Britain at the end of the fourth century (perhaps sometime around AD 384). His father Calpurnius was a Decurion, (a city counsellor who had to be a landowner of at least 16 acres). Decurians were described as the 'sinews of the Roman Empire' by one historian. Caplurnius was also a deacon in the Christian Church, and his father Potitus, Patrick's grandfather, was a priest or presbyter.

Patrick's entry into this world coincided with a period of overwhelming change and upheaval. The power and stability of Rome was fading. The western half of the empire, already in terminal decline, was rapidly accelerating to the point of complete collapse. The old order would soon vanish leaving a vacuum into which a new darkness would rush. The atmosphere was charged with uncertainty. Uncertainty is the mother of fear and instability and the volatile conditions then prevailing would soon lend themselves to an implosion that would shake the foundations of civilisation to its core.

Emperor Theodosius (347-395) ruled the empire when Patrick was born. He had crushed several attempts to usurp him and successfully dealt with various other attacks that threatened the borders of his realm. However, upon his death his power passed into lesser hands and troubles that had once been irritations flared up into major crises. In AD 376, the Huns had created a refugee problem of huge proportions as vast numbers of Goths fled before this fearsome foe spilling across the Danube into Theodosius' Empire. Although they were absorbed to a degree, the seeds were sown for later disaster when Alaric the Goth, who was also a Roman General, turned against his masters. He led an army of disgruntled Goths into the heart of Rome, sacking the 'eternal city' in AD 410 much to the horror of its bewildered inhabitants. Three years previously, on New Year's Eve AD 406, the Vandals, Sueves, and Alans had poured across the Rhine, sweeping through Gaul and Spain. In order to deal with these escalating threats the Roman legions in Britain were withdrawn in phases to bolster defences on the continent. As they vanished (the last remnants finally leaving in AD 409), Britain's border and coastal regions became vulnerable to raids and attacks from Ireland.

I can hear echoes of Theoden's speech in *Lord of the Rings* before the Battle for Helm's Deep as he lamented, 'Where is the horse and the rider? Where is the horn that was blowing? They have passed like rain on the mountains. Like wind in the meadow. The days have gone down in the

West, behind the hills, into shadow... How did it come to this?'

This was the world into which Patrick was born. How did his mother fare in labour I wonder? Was it long, drawn out and painful? A foreshadowing of her own son's future hardship? We will never know. But one thing of which we can be certain is that as the infant Patrick began to live, Rome as an empire began to die. And with each laboured breath it echoed the words in woeful lament, 'Ichabod, the glory has departed!'

The ground of the western empire was being shaken by the thundering hooves of the approaching horses of the Apocalypse. These ghostly beasts of impending ruin tore up the turf as they raced towards its startled citizens, who were unprepared for what was to come and quite powerless to stop it. The awful temptation to live in denial was ever present. People continued to see in the familiar symbols of Rome's past glories a false security. The lingering echoes of its once powerful voice, long since silent, provided the necessary permission to bury their heads in the sand. Like children who place their hands over their eyes thinking themselves invisible and safe, they refused to see.

The unfolding nightmare of Barbarian rule and destruction spread like a dark storm cloud over the Roman provinces. It gained momentum, unleashing its withering ferocity upon the inhabitants of the lands. The flickering flame of classical antiquity with its refinement and learning was extinguished and Europe plunged headlong into the abyss of the Dark Ages.

But such is the power of providence, that God will move with such strength through one surrendered life so as to change things forever. The Almighty shall have His way and men shall bow. Thus around AD 400 God's eye was fixed upon an unremarkable sixteen year old boy, Patrick, living somewhere near the vulnerable British coastline and oblivious to the approach of an Irish raiding party from across the Irish Sea. And then it happened! Innocence and malice collided. Snatched from his home and all that he loved he was forced into brutal Irish slavery! God, however began to work in His young protégé immediately with patience and skill. Concealed within a Celtic darkness God hid Patrick until he was ready. Then after six long years of harsh servitude, as suddenly as he had been taken, he vanished from his slave master's custody and escaped. Decades later, by the Spirit's leading he would to return to the land of his captivity, landing at Strangford Lough, Co. Down in AD 432. By the time of his death, circa AD 461, such a change had been wrought that the island of Ireland would never be the same again. Nor for that matter, would the rest of the world.

Prayer

Father, I pray that Jesus would be glorified in our lives as we journey with Patrick. Lead us and guide us Holy Spirit. Mould us, shape us, fashion us into weapons of righteousness in the hand of our Lord and King. Prepare us and equip us for the days ahead, for things shall not remain as they are for much longer, they shall surely change and we must be ready, for we were born for such a time as this. Amen.

For further reading:

1 Corinthians 1:27-29; Zechariah 4:6

CHAPTER TWO

CAPTIVITY

'When I was about sixteen I knew not the one true God. I was captured and brought to Ireland as were many thousands of others. We had turned from God, not keeping His laws nor heeding His servants who declare to us His salvation. It was the Lord's doing that He might reveal to me my unbelief that I should turn from my sins and be converted.' *St Patrick*

It began the same as every other day but by nightfall nothing would ever be the same again. The writer of Proverbs had well said, 'Do not boast about tomorrow, for you do not know what a day may bring forth.' (Proverbs 27:1 NKJV). Patrick was to learn that truth and his experience drove him to seek God every waking hour of every day for the rest of his life.

Born into nobility Patrick enjoyed a privileged upbringing. He was raised in a beautiful home environment, growing up in a villa with servants in an unidentified place lost to history by the name of Bennavem Taburniae. There he enjoyed a good education with prospects of succeeding his father as owner of the estate. But privilege can breed arrogance and arrogance, complacency. Responsibility is passed over while a 'living for the moment' philosophy is pursued with missionary zeal. Little, if any thought, is given to the future. It becomes not so much 'seize the day' as squander the day. Why is it that we value things most when we've lost them? Or in Patrick's case, been taken from them.

The decision by Irish tribesmen to cross the Irish Sea to plunder people and possessions was made purely out of greed and a desire for callous gain. The illegitimate accumulation of wealth brought the ruthless much power and formidable reputations. Titles like 'Niall of the Nine Hostages' give us a glimpse into this terrifying world. That others suffered was irrelevant to the pagan Celtic mind. Mammon not mercy was king.

When Patrick was taken, his captors would have held a triage. The old, the weak and the sick were to be slaughtered on the spot. Only the young, strong and able were taken. Enchained, with an iron collar around the neck, those 'fortunate' to have been chosen were bundled into boats bound for Ireland. Patrick's last memories of home were probably the cries and moans of the dying. The fetid smell of blood and the acrid aroma of burning homes must have filled the air. The waking nightmare had only just begun. Communication from captor to captive was reduced to shouts in Irish, a foreign tongue to Patrick, and beatings with fists and clubs to ensure the instant submission and compliance of the human cargo. Education, privileged upbringing and titles were rendered worthless in an instant. The place of these prospective slaves was firmly at the bottom of the food chain, no longer persons but possessions without rights.

One can only imagine the kind of emotional concussion experienced by Patrick and his fellow slaves. Such traumas are not quickly overcome as David noted with pain in one of his Psalms.

'Out of the depths I have cried to You, O Lord;

Lord, hear my voice!

Let Your ears be attentive

To the voice of my supplications.'

(Psalms 130:1-2 NKJV).

When the storm hits, we instinctively look for shelter. When the tempest struck Patrick's world he reached to the One whom he had formerly rejected. With his emotions overwhelmed, fear and confusion threatened to consume him; he had to take stock fast.

It is important for us to realise that emotions do not equal outcome. Great figures of the Bible fought discouragement and depression; Elijah, Moses, Peter and the disciples among them. All these suffered terribly in the emotional realm. The Apostle Paul once lamented, 'For we do not want you to be ignorant, brethren, of our trouble which came to us in Asia: that we were burdened beyond measure, above strength, so that we despaired even of life.' (2 Corinthians 1:8 NKJV). Churchill, the British wartime leader who galvanised a nation, mobilised it for war and on to victory in the face of impossible odds, told of his 'Black Dog' that followed him, namely depression.

When we are confronted with a crisis, the very first thing to do is acknowledge that our emotional reaction is a natural one. We must try to set our emotions to one side and be prepared to live with the inner turmoil for a while. Emotions, remember, do not equal outcome.

Next we must find our fixed point. Those who navigate at night in the great outdoors look for Polaris in the night sky. This is the North Star and it always remains in the same position. This is a fixed point that allows a person to identify the direction in which they are travelling. Thus, finding their bearings, they move on. As a believer in Christ, difficult though it is, we must believe that God is ultimately in control. God is our fixed point. Trials come and trials go but God remains, faithful and immoveable. Making sense of things at the time can be all but impossible. Looking back we may be able to trace the rainbow through the rain. But whether or not this is so, we can always say our time is in His hand. We can choose to believe and 'know that all things work together for good to them that love God, to them that are the called according to His purpose.' (Romans 8:28 KJV).

Some may object and say, you have no idea what I'm going through, so you can't say that. Perhaps that's true, but we cannot accuse Patrick of having a cloistered existence and so he is qualified to say exactly that about his own bitter experience. He describes how his own captivity was used by God for his good.

> 'We had turned from God not keeping His laws nor heeding his servants who declared to us his salvation. **It was the Lord's doing** that he might reveal to me my unbelief that I should turn from my sins and be converted...'

The same Apostle Paul who recounted that he 'despaired of life,' also wrote optimistically, 'No temptation has overtaken you except such as is common to man; but God is faithful, who will not allow you to be tempted beyond what you are able, but with the temptation will also make the way of escape, that you may be able to bear it.' (1 Corinthians 10:13 NKJV).

Patrick saw God through the mist of his present misery, and looking up, found his fixed point. Though his emotions were in free fall he had made his first and most important choice, to seek God regardless of what befell him. You and I must do the same. When we have nowhere else to go we must turn to the One to whom we should have gone at first. Having turned to God as his fixed point what did Patrick choose to do next? We shall see in the following chapter.

Prayer

Father in the midst of trial, hide me in the secret of Your presence. When the storms of life blow hard, shield me from the tempest. I turn to You and declare in the words of Isaiah, 'Behold, God is my salvation; I will trust, and not be afraid: for The Lord Jehovah is my strength and my song; He also is become my salvation.' (Isaiah 12:2 KJV). In trials make a way of escape, suffer me not to endure beyond what I can bear but in all things reveal the hidden strength of Christ in me, that having done all to stand I may stand. Father, I know that all things don't come from You, but all things can be used by You for good. Let me draw inspiration from Your servant Joseph who said to his brothers, 'But as for you, you thought evil against me; but God meant it for good, to bring to pass as it is this day, to save much people alive.' (Genesis 50:20 KJV)

Fortify me, strengthen me, I pray with might in the inner man. I choose to rejoice in the midst of pain, for You O Lord will bring great deliverance and victory and I will be stronger.

For further reading:

Romans 8:28; Genesis 50:20

CHAPTER THREE

THE ANVIL - CRYING OUT

'Once in Ireland, I daily looked after sheep and praying throughout each day the love and fear of God increased within me and my faith was strengthened. And being moved in Spirit upon the mountains and in the woods I prayed up to one hundred times in the morning and as much at night. Arising to pray a great while before day whether in snow or frost or rain I experienced no ill effects neither laziness as the Spirit within me was strong then...' *St Patrick*

Patrick, as a slave, prayed upwards of two hundred prayers a day upon the mountain slopes and foothills. Spread over the six year period of his captivity that equated to almost half a million prayers. His place of captivity became the anvil upon which European Christianity was fashioned.

His prayers were not dry liturgical, meaningless repetitions but deep charismatic expressions of a soul searching for and crying out to God. His example should be an encouragement to us all in our times of greatest difficulty, for it is then that we need to press deeper into God.

Such was the harshness of Irish slavery that the average life expectancy of a slave was thirty years. Escape was all but impossible and, if attempted, failure to reach freedom had dire consequences. A captured fugitive could expect a severe punishment beating at the very least, but more likely, execution. A slave was the property of his or her master.

Considering these dark facts, how easy and probable it was for one who fell into such misfortune to slip into a whirlpool of bitterness and self pity. The sucking quicksand of misfortune threatening always to swallow its prey alive until the individual became a living corpse. Programmed to function by constant threat of punishment the individual would perform the tasks while emotionally numb. A world filled with pain and a world devoid of meaning.

Yet not so with Patrick. In losing his freedom he had found his God. Materially destitute yet spiritually rich. But lest we think after some romantic fashion that this was a simple or natural step for him to take, we must think again. Patrick enjoyed no 'head start' in the way of faith, for by his own admission he had rejected it. As a godless young man he could have said, 'See there is no God after all. If there was, how could He let this happen to me?' He chose not to. Instead he chose to find the One he had shunned. Patrick prayed from the start and never stopped till the day he died.

A thousand years earlier king David had composed the lyrics to the song of Patrick's heart, during his own wilderness time.

> 'O God, You are my God;
> Early will I seek You;
> My soul thirsts for You;
> My flesh longs for You
> In a dry and thirsty land
> Where there is no water.
> So I have looked for You in the sanctuary,
> To see Your power and Your glory.
> Because Your lovingkindness is better than life,
> My lips shall praise You.
> Thus I will bless You while I live;
> I will lift up my hands in Your name.
> My soul shall be satisfied as with marrow and fatness,
> And my mouth shall praise You with joyful lips.
> When I remember You on my bed,
> I meditate on You in the night watches.
> Because You have been my help,
> Therefore in the shadow of Your wings I will rejoice.
> My soul follows close behind You;
> Your right hand upholds me.
> But those who seek my life, to destroy it,
> Shall go into the lower parts of the earth.
> They shall fall by the sword;
> They shall be a portion for jackals.
> But the king shall rejoice in God;
> Everyone who swears by Him shall glory;

> But the mouth of those who speak lies shall be stopped.'
> (Psalm 63 NKJV).

Patrick was now in the school of the Holy Spirit and his tutor would do a thorough job. God was preparing His man. Muirchu, Patrick's biographer of the seventh century, recounted 'the many visits of Victoricus (the angel sent to him by God)' during this time. This legend must not be quickly dismissed for such experiences are authenticated by Scripture itself.

> 'For He shall give His angels charge over you, to keep you in all your ways.'
>
> (Psalms 91: 11 NKJV).
>
> 'Are they not all ministering spirits sent forth to minister for those who will inherit salvation?'
>
> (Hebrews 1: 14 NKJV).

The Apostle Paul had known God's protective arm during his testing times and recalled, 'And He said unto me, My grace is sufficient for thee: for My strength is made perfect in weakness. Most gladly therefore will I rather glory in my infirmities, that the power of Christ May rest upon me.' (2 Corinthians 12: 9-10 NKJV).

No doubt Patrick began to experience this grace of God almost immediately. We too, must look to God for His grace when we are tested. But let us be clear about one thing. In this 'instant' age we expect challenges to be resolved immediately so we can get on with life. God often has other ideas. He will allow the process of the ordeal to perfect us, to bring us to maturity. One of my least favourite scriptures is found in the Book of James. Here he teaches about how to profit from trials.

> 'My brethren, count it all joy when you fall into various trials, knowing that the testing of your faith produces patience. But let patience have its perfect work, that you may be perfect and complete, lacking nothing.' (James 1: 2-4 NKJV).

For Patrick, without the ordeal there would have been no ordination. It is the same for you and me. It is the process of having to walk through each trial that makes us grow in God. Every foundry has its own furnace; the place where steel is tempered and made strong. Tempering is a heat treatment technique applied to ferrous alloys, such as steel or cast iron, to achieve greater toughness by decreasing the hardness of the alloy. The reduction in hardness decreases the brittleness of the metal. In the intense heat of adversity, our hearts, by God's grace, are softened and become less brittle. Therefore we are no longer as prone to snap under pressure.

Prayer

O Lord, You are the God of Abraham, Isaac, and Jacob, You are the God of Joseph and Joshua, You are the God of David and Daniel. You are the One who strengthens and anoints in the midst of adversity. Pour out upon me Your servant, a spirit of supplication and intercession. That the streams of living water would flow from within me even in the dry places of life. That I would feel the pulse of Your life beating through mine. You O Lord, who fed Elijah by the Brook Cherith, feed my spirit and strengthen my soul even as I pray without ceasing. Light a fire within me that will never be extinguished!

For further reading:

2 Corinthians 12:9-10

CHAPTER FOUR

DREAMS AND VISIONS

'As I lay sleeping a voice came to me in the night saying, 'It is good that you fast for you are soon to return home.' And a little while later I heard a voice speak, 'Look your boat is prepared.' It was some two hundred miles away, at a place I had never visited, neither did I know anyone there. I fled, parting from the man with whom I had been for six years. Being led by God I went in His strength until I reached that boat I was afraid of nothing.' *St Patrick*

The precise location of Patrick's captivity is disputed. One strong possibility is the area of Mount Slemish in County Antrim, Northern Ireland. This extinct volcano rises from the surrounding terrain with forbidding domination. A small mountain in stature yet dark and imposing upon a fresh young slave. Did he see this extinct volcano as a symbol of his own extinguished innocence? Was its hidden message to him one of the immoveable and unforgiving nature of his predicament? Visible yet dead inside? Whatever lonely thoughts crossed his bewildered mind they were of little comfort. Still grace, that welcome intruder, found its way into Patrick's heart almost uninvited. As we have seen already, its fruit was clearly evident as he forsook all self pity and displayed an outrageous trust in God.

This was no passive trust, however. It would seem from Patrick's own account that he had actively pursued a disciplined life of prayer and fasting. Now it seems he had an angelic visitation, for the voice had said, 'It is well that you fast.' Was this the angel Victoricus that Muirchu had described? Earlier Patrick had recounted his almost obsessive practice of prayer, day and night, night and day. This apparent addiction to God developed as a result of habit, and that habit was a result of choice. Whether it came easy to him or not we cannot tell. What we do know is that it paid off!

Patrick now experienced a direct communication from heaven regarding God's immediate plans for his future – escape! This was the first glimmer of hope he had received in six years. The message for us here is clear: 'be disciplined in seeking God and for heaven's sake persevere!'

Keeping close to God and not giving up can

be a tall order when you're in the thick of things and can't see a way through. During such times the days roll relentlessly on and threaten to smother hope like the haystack hides the needle. This is when we need to put one spiritual foot in front of the other and keep going.

The Celts believed that dead relatives spoke to them through dreams and so spent nights by a grave in order to hear from a deceased loved one. Patrick's dream was not of that source, though it is likely many of his family had perished in the raid that led to his captivity. Speaking with the dead is a practice forbidden in the Bible. Dreams and visions however, are commonplace in the stories of scripture. Joseph, Mary's betrothed was warned several times in a dream in order to protect Jesus from King Herod's murderous intent. On the day of Pentecost Peter reminded his listeners of God's own promise as recorded by the Prophet Joel,

> 'And it shall come to pass in the last days, saith God, I will pour out of My Spirit upon all flesh: and your sons and daughters shall prophesy, and your young men shall see visions, and your old men shall dream dreams.' (Acts 2: 17 KJV).

Patrick decided to act. He had spent long enough getting to know God and now the Heavenly Father had spoken. No 'farewells' and no leaving party, just a slipping away into the night perhaps, after making the necessary preparations. To say that this was a bit risky is a monumental understatement. He was now a fugitive and if captured could expect no mercy. At best he would have been severely beaten within an inch of his life but most likely executed.

There are times in life when the difficult choices have to be made and the question becomes, is God at the centre of our decision making process? For Patrick this was a definite 'Yes!' His practice of prayer and fasting had formed an inner sensitivity to God's leading. Now that the way forward was clear the greater risk was to stay put. Time and hardship would eventually exact their remorseless toll leading to a premature death. On the other hand, was he being led to destiny or disaster? Taking that first step of faith is never easy. It takes courage and like Peter we can step out of the boat only to lose our nerve and begin to sink, but making a choice not to take it can lead to a lifetime of regret, and the 'kingdom' of regret is ruled by that tyrant of memory which forever mocks us saying, 'Look what could have been if only you had ... '

Patrick had made his choice. He thrust himself into the unknown and into a wilderness of a thousand dangers. Pagan Ireland was dark and brutal. It was also governed by the mysterious powers of the druids. When he stepped out, the very air Patrick breathed was thick with magic and menace. What was to become of him?

Embarking on a new career as a fugitive is a risky business. For Patrick, as we have seen, the prospect of capture was bleak. Aren't we all fugitives? To be sure we are not all fleeing from physical slavery, but every Christian has left his or her own Egyptian bondage of sin and old ways and habits pursue us every day. Let's be clear, when Patrick left his slave master he stepped forward with courage, he did not flee as a coward. God had called him out of slavery and into freedom. Nevertheless he had to fight for that freedom and travel with wisdom.

Patrick's escape route was fraught with danger. First, the terrain posed its own unique challenges. It comprised thick forests with rivers that criss-crossed the land. Roads were made of wood which overlaid dangerous marshland and bogs. To stray from these primitive paths was to risk drowning or suffocation by being sucked into the soft, dark, stinking earth. But to stay on the road Patrick risked capture. One ancient Greek traveller, Philemon, recorded that it took twenty days to cross Ireland from East to West as he made a journey of some 150 miles. Patrick told us that his journey was 200 miles, which meant he journeyed probably for well over a month perhaps living off the land. He would have needed to avoid settlements and communities at all costs.

Accustomed as he was to a life of prayer, one can imagine that his rigorous practice of that discipline deepened as he depended upon God as never before to provide and protect. Only prayer can afford the peace and strength required to continue in such extreme circumstances. Patrick testified, 'Being led by God, I went in His strength until I reached the boat I was afraid of nothing.'

I think here, of several examples of angels intervening to free imprisoned servants of God in the Bible. The Apostles were sprung from prison through angelic powers (See Acts 5: 18-20). Elsewhere, when Peter was escorted out of jail by the hand of an angel who led and protected him (See Acts 12: 6-10). I'm sure the angels were present with Patrick also. He claimed to have no fear. Was he escorted by Victoricus perhaps?

Patrick's destination may have been a harbour in Wexford and some have favoured summertime being the most likely season as sailing was thought to be difficult around the Irish coast in winter. This last part of his journey was the most dangerous. His foreign accent and poor Irish would have identified him as a fugitive slave. When he found and approached the ship he would have been exposed and vulnerable.

Not surprisingly he was initially refused access by the captain. This was dangerous. He prayed as he walked away. He always prayed about everything, never giving up. Almost immediately one of the crew called him back and said the captain had reconsidered and was willing to take him on board. The sailors then invited him to participate in a pagan custom before boarding to show good faith. Here lies Satan's subtlety, the offer to compromise one's faith to gain that which is desired.

Having come so far and passed through so many dangers unscathed, Patrick was almost within reach of his goal. Boarding the very ship God had shown him in the dream was just a ritual away. How easy it would have been to let his guard slip. How easy it would have been to say, it's only a little thing to participate in this pagan ritual. After all they might refuse me passage if I don't.

Faced with such a choice the pressure was on. To refuse was to risk rejection and possible death. To accept would be a compromise that would ensure his passage but give Satan a hold on his life. What to choose? How many of us have faced predicaments like this? A test of faith and integrity. In those seconds before he made his choice the adrenaline must have surged through Patrick's veins. His heart now beating in his mouth threatening to explode. Tremors beginning to weaken his legs. 'No!' he said, 'My faith in Jesus Christ forbids me to do that.' Relief... He had passed the test and this moment lay in the hands of God alone. But the silence! The deafening silence as the eyes of the sailors bored into him whilst they processed what he had said. After what must have seemed like an eternity the crew relented, being happy that he greeted them in a manner appropriate to his own faith. He stepped onto the boat with its cargo of Irish wolfhounds bound for Amorica, modern day France. Patrick was free. The ship's crew had an extra pair of hands. All were happy. The shores of the past receded gradually from view but the coastline of his future had yet to appear. What did it hold? He didn't know, only that he had reached the point of no return. A blessing or a curse? To trust God is never a curse.

Prayer

Father, I thank You for the supernatural provision of angels in my life, that You have given them to me to serve Your purposes. Thank you that Your ministering spirits, Your flames of fire are all around me, who am an heir of salvation. Release Your Holy Angels to act on my behalf, O God. I believe they are active right now in every circumstance.

For further reading:

Acts 5:18-20; Acts 12:6-10; 2 Kings 6:17

CHAPTER FIVE

PROVISION

'Three days later we made land. Travelling through desolation for twenty-eight days they had no food and hunger raged within them. Finally the boat's captain said, 'Answer me this Christian, you tell us that your God is great and all powerful, why will you not pray for us? We perish from hunger and may see no living soul again.' Boldly I told them, 'Turn to the Lord my God with your whole heart, for with Him nothing is impossible, that today He may supply more than enough food for your journey for He has ample store everywhere.' And so with God's aid it came to pass; at once a herd of pigs appeared before us right in front of our eyes. Killing many they camped two nights regaining their strength, even their dogs which had become weak and lifeless were satisfied. From that moment they had ample food...' *St Patrick*

The ship Patrick had boarded took three days to cross the sea from the Irish harbour to a port in Brittany. (Such a journey was recently re-enacted using a replica vessel similar to that of Patrick's period). Having made land, he recounted how they traversed a wilderness or desert for twenty-eight days. This seems a strange description of Gaul's geography, leading some to ask whether this is just symbolism of some sort. However we can eliminate any mystery by appealing to the facts of history. On 31st of December 406 Barbarians invaded Gaul and according to the historian J B Bury:

> 'The devastation to the extensive provinces and the conquered cities of Gaul was terrible; contemporary writers of prose and verse alike complain bitterly of the atrocities committed by the Barbarians in this unhappy country. The oldest people could not remember so disastrous an invasion.' (Cambridge Medieval History, Macmillan, 1911, p266).

Given the huge numbers of the invading forces, their requirement for food and sustenance would have been substantial, stripping the land bare. This coupled with the ruthless brutality meted out, makes it easy to picture a post-apocalyptic landscape here. Wandering through such a barren and hostile environment would have been treacherous. With food being scarce, it is likely that strangers would have been greeted with suspicion and even hostility. There is an aura of the movie 'Mad Max' about it.

It is one thing to profess the Christian faith in the leafy middle class areas of suburbia. It is quite another to practise it in places of dark foreboding or within a twilight world of uncertainty and threat. Yet this is precisely where faith must come alive, whether it is beneath the creeping shadow of extremist threat or in the heart of inner city Belfast, or North America, amid the simmering tensions of a divided community that frequently erupt in uncontrolled violence.

In Patrick's story we see the boldness of his authenticity displayed. Hunger raged amongst the ship's crew and the eyes of the malcontent turned toward this former slave as the captain demanded proof of his profession. It is said that on a windy day a rotten apple discovers itself. On this particular 'windy day' was there a rottenness to Patrick's faith? That's what these hardened sailors wanted to know. The American statesman Benjamin Franklin famously remarked that 'Well done is better than well said!' But isn't that the whole point?

True faith looks for an opportunity to shine on the stage of adversity. And it shines in many different colours before an audience of the hurting and the helpless, before the critics with their doubts and atheism. It may shine with the colour of public forgiveness from a father towards his daughter's killers who extinguished her life with a mindless terrorist bomb (It has been observed that no flag is ever large enough to cover the shame of killing the innocent). It may shine through the sheer lifelong determination of a William Wilberforce who spends himself to obtain justice for the oppressed. It may shine with the colour of quiet courage displayed in one who trusts God to order and provide following the doctor's report.

Wherever faith shines, its beams attract the weary eye's attention amidst the blackness of this world's night and guides it to a greater power than we mere mortals possess. Yes we are to be His witnesses in this world. Someone once said, 'Preach the gospel always, use words if you have to.' What the sailors really wanted to know was this, 'Patrick, is your God real?' Patrick prayed and God answered. God can look after his own reputation well enough but invites us to be His ambassadors, His representatives on earth. We are to be sign posts, always fixed in our pointed direction, not weather vanes changing with each adverse wind.

Faith displays a certainty that this world needs, but let's remember that faith does not have all the answers but rather trusts the One who has. Faith never rides roughshod over the views and positions of others, it simply refuses to yield to the whirlpool of hopelessness in the raging sea of other people's doubt. Faith never says 'I have it all together!' Rather it says, "I can do all things through Christ who gives me strength. And what He's done for me he can do for you too.'

Patrick didn't claim to be anything other than a broken individual made whole by God. He always boasted in God never about himself. Yet at the same time he refused to shrink back when circumstances demanded his voice and action as Christ's representative. He also publically trusted God to provide for his own and others' needs. How does his example embolden you?

Prayer

Dear Lord, forgive me for ever doubting You. All through Your Word You proclaim that You will provide for Your children. Your Word says, 'I have been young, now I am old; yet I have not seen the righteous forsaken, nor his seed begging for bread.' (Psalm 37:25 KJV). I put my trust in You for you are Jehovah Jireh, The Lord who sees and provides. There is no need that is too great for You, no mountain too high. I call upon You now Lord of Hosts to send Your provision now. I will bless you at all times, Your praise will continually be in my mouth. You are my Shepherd, I'll not want. Thank You that Your goodness and mercy shall follow me all the days of my life … Amen.

For further reading:

Philippians 4:19; Psalm 84:11,

Psalm 34:10

CHAPTER SIX

MESSENGERS OF SATAN

'That same night whilst sleeping, Satan tormented me fiercely, which shall remain in my mind to the end of my days. It was as though he fell upon me like a massive bolder so that I could not move my limbs at all. But how did I come to call upon Elias as unlearned as I am? As I shouted, 'Elias, Elias,' I saw the sun rise in the sky and at once the magnificent brightness of that sun shone on me. Immediately all oppression fled and I was free. It is my belief that I was upheld by Christ the Lord with His Spirit groaning on my behalf.' *St Patrick*

'Come to Jesus and all your troubles shall disappear!' Sounds wonderful doesn't it? It is, however, untrue. Those who make such claims know neither the Scriptures nor the Saviour. Jesus never made such promises. His honesty and His kindness were shown by telling His closest followers that in this world we shall have tribulation and trials. The Apostle Paul penned the phrase, 'Fight the good fight of faith.' (1 Timothy 6:12). In fact Paul did not stop fighting until his death at the hands of Roman executioners. He explicitly instructed the Christians in Ephesus to 'Be strong in the Lord and the power of His might,' (Ephesians 6:10), whilst they 'wrestled' with the dark powers of the evil one; to be especially careful to wear the 'whole armour of God'. Practical advice for practising Christians.

Patrick's account of this Satanic attack is unsettling to say the least. He is at pains to stress the lasting effect it had on him. Clearly he was traumatised. But he was also victorious. The two are not incompatible in Christian faith and experience. We are not robots. We are sentient creatures who can experience trauma and yet see ourselves as victors rather than victims.

See Christ sweating great drops of blood at Gethsemane. Scientists tell us that this only occurs when someone is in a state of extreme stress. Yet it was in this place of traumatic wrestling that the battle of Calvary was won by Christ before it had even begun. The secret, therefore of our surviving the attacks of Satan is to root our response and recovery in God, specifically the person of the Lord Jesus Christ. To borrow a phrase, we 'hide ourselves in His wounds.' We overcome Satan by the blood of the Lamb and the word of our testimony (Revelation

12:11). Patrick testifies that throughout his encounter with the dark powers it was his belief that he was 'upheld by Christ the Lord with His Spirit groaning' within on his behalf. Christ promised never to abandon His own.

What was the source of this attack Patrick experienced? Certainly it was demonic but how was it brought to bear upon this young man? We must remember that everything supernatural that occurs in this world must have the permission and cooperation of man. 'The heaven, even the heavens, are the Lords: but the earth hath He given to the children of men.' (Psalm 115:16 KJV). That's why we must pray before we see God move. That is also how Satan gained control of this world, by the permission and cooperation of our first parents. That is why God had to incarnate himself and become a man to rescue mankind. Even this was only made possible as God spoke through his servants the Prophets, men who saturated the earth's atmosphere with the declared intent of God; voices preparing the way of the Lord.

It is the human voice that facilitates the supernatural powers on earth. Therefore what tongue lay behind this demonic visitation Patrick experienced? Possibly a druid's, one who knew

Patrick's master in Ireland and who was sought to utter a curse against this Christian fugitive who dared to trust in his God and defy the old order. It's just a theory but a plausible one nonetheless.

How does Patrick respond? He cries out, 'Elias, Elias.' This is puzzling. Why would he call upon an Old Testament figure? He explains that it was Christ's Spirit groaning within that prompted this cry. Why would Christ do this? If we translate the meaning of the name Elias we find it is the Greek rendering of Elijah which means 'Jehovah is God'. What Patrick is actually declaring is that Jehovah, not Satan, is God. The 'spell' is broken and the defeat of the powers of darkness is symbolised by the resplendent sunrise. This was a straightforward, practical lesson in spiritual warfare during 'on the job' training. As unpleasant as it was for Patrick, never again would he be in any doubt about the supremacy of God's power.

Prayer

Lord, there are times when I feel overwhelmed by such oppression that I wonder whether I can continue the path You have laid before me. But I know that I shall endure and overcome when words fail me to pray as I ought; there in the midst of the Satanic onslaught Your Spirit takes over, groaning deep within me. In the silence let me feel Your powerful hidden currents begin to flow within me, welling up and bursting forth like a volcanic eruption of intercession, sweeping all away in the molten lava of your Spirit.

For further reading:

Matthew 4:10-11; 1 Peter 5: 6-11

CHAPTER SEVEN

MACEDONIAN CALL

'A few years later I was reunited with my family in Britain. Receiving me as a son they pleaded with me that now after so much adversity and trial I should leave them no more. But there I saw a night vision of a man. His name was Victoricus appearing as if he were coming from Ireland with innumerable letters. He passed one to me and I read the beginning of the letter which said: 'The Voice of the Irish'; and as I read those words I perceived that I heard their voice at the same time – they were those beside the Wood of Voclut adjacent to the Western Sea. Their cry was with one voice, 'Holy boy we ask you to come and walk among us again.' Thank God after many years He granted their request.'
St Patrick

When a person leaves the past behind they have not yet discovered their future. Patrick tells us that a few years passed from the time of his escape before he was reunited with his family. Within that time he was taken captive again. It is likely that word got out on their travels that he was an escaped slave with six years' experience.

He was trained and hardy. Useful to those who had lost valuable manpower in the great Barbarian invasion, perhaps, or even a Barbarian entrepreneur with an eye for a quick profit.

One can hardly imagine the sense of demoralisation Patrick must have felt. He had left the frying pan only to land in the fire. How many times do we think a thing is over only to encounter another setback? 'Hope deferred makes the heart sick.' No doubt Patrick's heart was sicker than most. Questions begin to surface at such times. 'Where was God this time?' 'Did I miss something? A warning or an instruction?' 'Is God angry with me?'

God spoke during the first night of this fresh incarceration: 'You will be with them two months.' Sixty nights later God delivered him from his captor's hands. We don't know how, just that He did. What was the purpose of all of this hardship and heartache? We can speculate that Patrick preached the gospel to his captors in much the same way Paul did when he was chained to his Roman guards just as God intended, but we do not have the facts.

What we do know is that 'all things work together for good to them that love God, to them who are the called according to His purpose.' (Romans 8:28 KJV); a scripture that is easy to read but more difficult to embrace when things seem to fall apart. But it is precisely such mysterious scriptures that afford the greatest hope and comfort. We don't have to be in control but just know that God is. There is nothing passive here. We can aggressively assert over and over in the midst of every trial, 'God is in control and this is working for good.' It is the very best antidote for that heart sickness of hopelessness because it brings us hope. 'When the desire cometh it is a tree of life.' (Proverbs 13:12 KJV). What desire? The God implanted desire that God's will be done to completion.

Seeing ourselves as servants of destiny rather than its masters is both healthy and wise. We begin to see ourselves not as the centre of the universe but as players on the world stage of the divine drama of redemption. We follow His script. We fight for His glory and the good of others according to His strategy. This becomes our tree of life that yields fruit in abundance.

Patrick's reunion with his family had not been expected following his kidnap and enslavement. Yet many years following that black and brutal day when the strangers came, here he was, home again.

I've often tried to imagine how it happened. According to some, his parents perished in the raid but Patrick talks about his people (probably relatives) receiving him back as a son. In my mind I see his silhouette on the horizon approaching a homestead. The occupants catching sight of this stranger who seems more and more familiar with every closing step. Then I hear the cries of astonishment that suddenly fill the air, 'Patrick! It's Patrick!' they shout as they realise who it is. I've pictured celebrations around the evening's fire stretching well into the night. Each face full of joy and wearing the warm glow of flames that cause even the shadows to dance in celebration of this son returned. Then as the embers die and one by one those gathered turn in for sleep, a solitary figure remains, alone with his thoughts but not lonely; for warmth and comfort and friendship and family have all converged this night, and conspired to grant a happy settled-ness that numbs all pain of his yesterdays. Hidden in the shadows, I see a young woman studying his frame, her eyes drawn to him as she ponders the image of one she knew and loved in that far away country they call the past. A line from a poem by W. B. Yeats runs through my mind, as though I heard the midnight breeze carry a whisper from her heart,

> 'But one … loved the pilgrim soul in you,
> And loved the sorrows of your changing face.'

I recently watched a news item showing Korean siblings in old age reunited for only a few hours. Separated during the Korean War, they now lived on either side of the border. It was heart breaking to see these precious people hold onto each other as raw emotions expressed what words could not. What made it even more painful was that these moments were stolen and could not last. Those few hours must have seemed like mere seconds. Fleeting and never to return. That was the last time they would see each other and they knew it. This was little more than a touching good-bye. Bittersweet to the taste and beyond their control. The wrenching pain of separation cannot be understood except by those who have experienced it. The choice had been made for them.

For Patrick, separation was a choice he would have to make. To be taken from your loved ones is painful but to leave your loved ones is possibly harder still for it is within your power to stay.

Patrick chose to leave and never return. How did it happen?

It seems that sometime after his return he began to experience dreams and night visions from God. In one vivid encounter he saw the man named Victoricus in the middle of the night hand him a letter and he heard voices too. What emotions must have swirled within! Was this a dream, vision or nightmare? Remember this wasn't a casual browse through a tourist brochure of Ireland replete with colour images of nightlife and breath-taking beauty that we might enjoy today. Not only was he reminded of the place he associated with misery and suffering, now he was being confronted with the sobering truth that God intended for him to return. Over three centuries earlier the Apostle Paul had been directed in a similar way having seen in a night vision a man of Macedonia urging him to come and help them. He promptly obeyed (see Acts 16: 6-10). This was Patrick's 'Macedonian call'.

The amount of energy needed for Patrick to process this startling revelation would have been immeasurable. It must have struck at the core of his being and shaken his foundations. But lest we empathise overly with Patrick let us view this from God's perspective. God is not shocked by anything, ever. David had a revelation of the mind of God which is sublimely and eloquently rehearsed in Psalm 139.

'All the days fashioned for me were written in your book when as yet there were none of them.' (Psalm 139: 16 NKJV).

Patrick's life had been already been mapped out for him. God had a purpose for his life. Circumstances had conspired first to unite Patrick with God, and second, to prepare him as an instrument for His purpose. There was a high call on Patrick's life, and that call would affect a nation and the world beyond. The late Welsh preacher Dr Martyn Lloyd-Jones said, 'The worst thing that can happen to a man is for him to succeed before he is ready.' Patrick's ordeal was all part of his preparation. God was not about to waste that. The high call was not going to be sacrificed for Patrick's personal comfort. It is not that God didn't care. No, quite the opposite. God had something far better for His young servant an opportunity to serve his Heavenly Master in the conversion of Ireland from Paganism and receive a rich heavenly reward.[1]

---

[1] Although Christianity in Ireland predated Patrick it spread rapidly following his arrival

It is sometimes difficult for us to comprehend God's overarching purpose for us. We are so taken with the immediacy of our felt needs that we fail to consider His grand scheme. Like a child who wishes to spend his week's pocket money all at once on something worthless instead of saving it up for something really valuable. Quite simply, we fail to understand the context of our existence. Ultimately we exist not for ourselves but for Him and those around us. Our lives should be seen as an investment to be poured into the world we inhabit. Instruments fashioned for the execution of His magnificent plan of redemption for humankind. Our lives are not our own but we are bought with a price (1Cor 6:20). This is not an easy thing to embrace. It requires a continual shift of thinking away from the self and towards Christ. I would suggest that it must be a discipline practised daily. One in which we fail more often than we care to think. Not so with Patrick.

He had attributed his captivity to his youthful rebellion. He saw in his hardship the hand of his Heavenly Father at work, bringing him to Christ and then drawing him into the deepest places of intimacy. To refuse this commission now could furnish nothing good. After all, perhaps Patrick reasoned, hadn't that been Jonah's problem? A flat refusal to go to Nineveh followed by some very unpleasant experiences? Patrick had made that mistake once and he wasn't about to repeat it. But I am convinced that the greater motivation was compassion rather than a fear of consequences, for thinking of his fellow slaves and the Irish he recalls, 'Thank God after many years he granted their request' for him to return. I think Patrick had found a friendship with God that he prized above all else, together with a love for the oppressed and even the oppressors. Now his greatest task was to inform his friends and family that he would be leaving. Heart-breaking!

Prayer

Father, I thank You that You have a plan for my life. Help me to see that all things so far – whatever I have experienced have shaped and prepared me for what is to come. Your Word says that there is a time and season to every purpose under heaven. I yield myself to Your timing and when You call I will be ready. Order my steps and direct my paths. O God guide me with Your eye. Let me hear Your voice behind me say, 'This is the way walk in it!' May Christ be in my eyes and in my seeing. May Christ be in my mouth and in my speaking. May Christ be in my heart and in my understanding.

For further reading:

Acts 16:7-10; Jeremiah 1:4-5

CHAPTER EIGHT

PRAYING IN THE SPIRIT

'On another occasion I saw Him praying within me. It was as though I was within my body and He was above me as I heard Him over my inner man where he prayed with powerful groanings. I was amazed and considered who this might be that prayed within me, however when His prayer finished He spoke telling me that He was the Spirit.' *St Patrick*

Few statements that Patrick made are as shocking or as comforting as this. Casual readers of scripture and nominal Christians will be startled by this confession. He describes witnessing a power that has taken up residence within him. A power that has knowledge, feelings and a will, all the marks of person-hood. This 'power/person' is within him and at the same time independent of him. Patrick is not in control here, but describes himself as an observer. Yet what Patrick describes is entirely scriptural. His experience is a fulfilment of Romans 8:26:

> 'Likewise the Spirit also helpeth our infirmities: for we know not what we should pray for as we ought: but the Spirit

itself maketh intercessions for us with groanings which cannot be uttered.' (KJV)

Like the musician who plays the instrument with such skill and beauty that we are left moved and speechless, we see God breathing through Patrick in prayer and it is wonderful to behold. Patrick has so yielded himself that he is supple in the Master's hands and sensitive to His touch. As the lathe becomes an extension of the woodworker, so Patrick has become an extension of Christ. We mustn't think of this as abnormal but rather as the norm. If we can't see it this way it is because we have placed the emphasis in our Christian life on dry ritual rather than a deepening relationship with Christ. We must focus on the person of Christ more than any set of practices. When we yield to Christ the person, He takes over. When we merely perform certain practices we retain control.

Patrick's experience followed a prolonged period of seeking God. By his own admission during slavery he had prayed hundreds of times each day in frost and rain. This had produced something special that went beyond mere acquaintance. Remember Jesus had said of Himself and the Father, 'I and the Father are one.' When we assess Jesus' prayer life we can easily see that there is a link between His frequent withdrawal to commune with His Father and the unity with Him that He demonstrated.

The Apostle Paul encouraged believers to become vessels of honour (2 Timothy 2:20). Vessels are to be filled and used in the service of the Householder. 'Christ is a Son over His own house; whose house are we ...' (Hebrews 3:6 KJV). Patrick was a filled vessel useful to the Master. He was filled with the Spirit and the Spirit was pleased to pray through this human vessel.

These 'groanings' of the Spirit Patrick experienced were intercessions according to the will of God, known, understood and answered by the Father (Romans 8:26-27). Given the magnitude of Patrick's assignment and just how dangerous it would be, the Spirit was making intercession for him and his work thus ensuring its success and his safety. We see clearly that what Patrick has described is not the ramblings of a half mad mystic, but rather that of a true son in the faith who is given wholly over to the service of God. Such intensity unsettles us only because we are content to paddle in the shallows of prayer and intimacy with God instead of launching into the deep. We can learn from Patrick that prolonged communion with God, cultivated day by day and developed over the years will yield treasures of fruit and favour beyond our imagination.

Prayer

Lord fill me afresh with Your Spirit, come, come... may a spirit of intercession fall on me, move through me Holy Spirit. Begin to groan deep within me. Let the fountains of the deep open up. Let the prayers that need to be prayed come forth shifting us into Your end-time purposes. Fashion me into a vessel of prayer. Bring to me the violent prayers, the forceful prayers that will see Your Kingdom advance.

For further reading:

Romans 8:26-27; Jude 20; Ephesians 5:18,19

CHAPTER NINE

PERSERVERANCE

'From the moment in my youth when I came to know Him the love and fear of God have increased within me and to this very day I thank God I have kept the faith through His grace. Every day I anticipate the prospect of being killed, cheated or enslaved. But I am not afraid of any of these things because of His promises. I have cast myself into the hands of Almighty God who sovereignly rules in all places.' *St Patrick*

To press onward, always onward. That should be the Christian's desire. How many of us do, consistently at least? We are tempted to stop, to quit. 'I wouldn't have started if I'd known what I was getting into.' Patrick had no such illusions. His faith was born in adversity. After his escape from captivity and when he had found peace and refuge once more amongst his kith and kin, he well understood the implication of Christ's call to return to Ireland when it came by the hand of Victoricus that night in the vision. There was no bubble to burst, no soft focus on the lens as he viewed his destiny. He simply counted the cost and went with his eyes wide open.

We have no account of the missing years between his call from God and his setting foot in Ireland again. His course was not a smooth one. Prolonged training in either Britain or Gaul, followed by waiting (It may have been over two decades before he began his mission). Accusations followed him from other servants of God who questioned the legitimacy of his ministry and his integrity following a betrayal by a close friend in whom he had confided about some sins of his youth. This continued to dog and discourage him as he lamented how he was 'attacked by a number of my seniors' who he said, 'brought up my sins.' The effect was devastating and he recalled how, 'on that day I was struck so that I might have fallen now and for eternity.' God, however, protected him despite these troubles and the threat of constant danger that accompanied him on the mission field, and he described how, 'the love and fear of God have increased within me.' That is the hallmark of maturity in Christ from one who has a job to do. Like Olympian Eric Liddell who said, 'When I run I can feel His pleasure,' Patrick sensed the pleasure of God as he served Him. This generated a deep sense of love and fear of God. When you love someone enough you'll do anything for them. But there was something more that attended Patrick's mission than just his inward disposition toward God and that was God's external manifest supernatural power.

Ireland had experienced a limited exposure to Christianity prior to Patrick's arrival, mainly through trade. But it seemed to accelerate following the start of his ministry. We must remember that Ireland was pagan to its core. The gods and goddesses of Celtic belief were the stuff of nightmares. The druids wielded tremendous power and respect within communities and tribes. Magic and superstition filled the air. So the question is why would the Irish so readily abandon the old way with its perceived power. The answer must be that Patrick demonstrated the greater power of God through the miraculous.

His time was so close to the Apostolic age that signs wonders and miracles were still a common occurrence. Augustine of Hippo (A near contemporary of Patrick) reported in his famous work 'City of God' that over seventy verifiable miracles had occurred in Hippo. Other early churchmen, including Clement of Alexandria and Irenaeus testified to healings and the dead being raised as being normal in the two centuries following the death of Christ's Apostles.

Power encounters between the servants of God and their pagan adversaries have passed into Celtic Christianity's folklore. Fantastical tales of God and His superior power in defeating the dark powers through various saints inspire awe in the telling. These have been preserved, passed down and no doubt exaggerated or invented by authors a thousand or so years ago who wished to emphasise the authority of their particular ecclesiastical site over others by appealing to their connection to a particular Celtic saint. Fact or fiction? What really matters is the importance attached to these stories in the cultural mind of a nation. These stories are valued and held forth as a heroic ideal to be embodied by other generations. A kind of gold standard in the realms of prayer, spiritual warfare and the spread of the Gospel. The trouble is that if the bar is set too high it becomes beyond our reach. With Patrick however, he is all too human; there is always a sense of, 'when I am weak, then I am strong' about him. Clear about his own infirmities yet aware of the power of Christ resting upon him.

It is in the context of Patrick's humanness that we can find our own motivation, because he was a man like us. I have no doubt that he moved profusely in the power of the supernatural whilst remaining a man like us. This same supernatural power won him admirers among the tribal ruling elite, of that I'm sure, for many were converted. But I'm also certain that it gained him many more powerful enemies, especially amongst the druids who saw their position threatened by this Christian. These druids would have used all their influence, craft and power to try and eliminate Patrick and his work. Which is why he daily expected capture or execution.

To persevere with such a threat hanging over him tells us something important about the man. It reveals that he was settled in his calling. He saw himself as having only one life to live and he had decided to spend that life, however long or short, for something better than life itself, God's glory and the good of men. Nothing else mattered. In this he was steadfast and immovable. This is the secret of all perseverance. A core fire conviction that what you are doing is not only right but also worth all the hardship experienced along the way. I don't believe that Patrick was a romantic or even an idealist. I think he was a realist with his feet firmly planted on the ground but one who had his eyes firmly fixed on the heavenly prize. One who knew that he would soon hear the voice of his Master speaking over him the thrilling words, 'Well done good and faithful servant. Come and share in your Masters happiness.'

Understanding this about Patrick should cause us to assess where we are right now in life. Have we left our 'First Love'? Are we, at this moment, making choices that are pleasing to God and which will yield an eternal reward? Do we still have that core fire within us that moves us to persevere amidst trial and opposition? If not why not? Patrick suffered more than most and yet pressed on joyfully proving that it is possible. There will always be ditches on either side of the road and we may fall in to them. When we do, the very best thing is to pick ourselves up, dust ourselves off and say, 'Oh well, I must be on my way.' Today is the first day of the rest of your life. Don't waste it wallowing in guilt, offence or past failure. Instead go straight to God and be washed clean from all of that stuff. You may have paused on your journey, and perhaps for a little too long, but there is a difference between pausing and packing it in. Press on pilgrim!

Prayer

Lord, thank You for the privilege of serving You, and for the opportunities that You bring my way. Father I recognise that there are spiritual adversaries that are opposed to Your kingdom advancing. Strengthen me I pray by Your Spirit in my inner man, that I may know your life and strength flowing within me. Let all discouragement be banished from my being and in the midst of adversity supply your joy to be my strength so that by You I can leap over every wall and run through every troop. I declare that You are my refuge and fortress and that I shall never be shaken. To live is Christ!

For further reading:

Romans 8:31; Acts 20:24 (KJV)

CHAPTER TEN

FINISHING THE COURSE

'Even if I wish to depart and return to Britain, for how much I have desired to see my country and parents and likewise the Lord's saints my brethren in Gaul, but the Spirit binds me and testifies within me that I would be wrong to leave, for I fear losing the fruits of my labour, or rather Christ's the Lord who beckoned me to come and remain with them till the end of my days.' *St Patrick*

'It is not the beginning, but the continuing of the same unto the end until it be thoroughly finished, which yieldeth the true glory.' These words of Francis Drake sum up Patrick's position. Having laboured so much and seen so much fruit there was the temptation to say, 'Well I've done enough and given the best years of my life to Ireland, now it's time to go back home and see out my days in peace and quietness with my family.' Had he done that, who could have faulted him? No serious observer could possibly object. The fact that he returned to Ireland at all was courageous and selfless, but he knew that to leave would be against God's wishes.

In the secret chambers of the heart, God speaks to His own. Often the conversations are private and the content is unknown to others. But we know what God has spoken and even if we can hide it from others, the echo of His voice always lingers with us. In the end I think it's not so much that judgement follows our refusals to God in the traditional sense of punishment meted out, but rather a gnawing sense of disappointment and regret. For Patrick this was his life's work. To cut that short wasn't just to miss out on a full reward in heaven, it ran the risk of losing the very fruits of his labour. Young saplings need tender care and protection. Patrick was responsible for that. In policing, presence is everything for 'presence' means prevention. Presence carries authority. How often do we refer to those who have impressed us as having 'presence'. When 'presence' is removed a vacuum remains that is quickly filled by something else.

If Patrick had left, his influential presence and protective authority would have gone too and the vacuum would have been filled by something else. Remember the druids? They would not have wasted the opportunity to regain their spiritual territory. Also there was the prospect of other corrupting influences being brought to bear upon the purity of the gospel. The Apostles had had to deal with such things, writing various letters to warn and strengthen the first believers as pagan and Christian beliefs began to merge in an unholy mixture.

We must never underestimate the lasting power of our presence in the world where we live and work. Being in God's will is more than just satisfying God by our unquestioning obedience. It's much more than that. It is about the fruit that is borne in the lives around us simply because we are present as salt and light. It is about the godly atmosphere we carry into the places where darker ones need to be displaced. It is about the prayers we can pray because we come by that crucial piece of information by being in the right place at the right time. And because of that we make a difference.

How often have we prayed, 'Thy will be done' when we really mean 'Thy mind be changed!'? We live in a consumer age where the customer is king and we carry that mind-set into our faith walk. God offers His products and we choose the best deal for us. Really? Is that how it works? Not according to the Bible. Ask Elijah. He chose to run away to Mount Horeb leaving his assignment unfinished following extreme pressure from

Jezebel. When he arrived God said, 'What are you doing here Elijah?' Others had to complete what he had started and was meant to finish. I'm sure that stayed with him for the rest of his earthly days. But it doesn't have to be that way.

We can learn from Patrick. He finished his course because he did three things. First, he learned intimacy with God. Second, he counted the cost of obedience before stepping out in obedience. He had no false expectation and no reason to be disappointed. Third, he maintained that intimacy with God, so that the love and fear of God grew stronger day by day and carried him through every danger and trial.

By the end of his life Patrick had laid a solid foundation for Christ in Ireland. It has been suggested that there were two to three hundred bishops and as many as three thousand priests as the fruit of his labours, not to mention the countless thousands of converts in a land of only two to three hundred thousand in population.

Over the next few centuries, in what became known as the golden age of Celtic Christianity, Patrick's spiritual sons and daughters 'swarmed like bees' across the European Continent planting monasteries and spreading the gospel. Patrick could not have foreseen that this would be the fruit of his choices. For him this was an unintended legacy. For God, however, this was His plan all along! I leave you with the wisdom of Proverbs 3: 5-6.

> 'Trust in the Lord with all thine heart; and lean not unto thine own understanding. In all thy ways acknowledge Him, and He shall direct thy paths.' (KJV).

Choose well, dear friend, and like Patrick follow that counsel. Countless others shall be eternally grateful to you that you did! Selah.

Prayer

Father, help me to see the big picture of a lifetime's service for Christ. Jesus glorified You by completing the work that You gave Him to do. Paul likewise spent himself for Your glory and for man's good. Father in Jesus Name I ask for the strength to complete my race. Equip me for every good work to do Your will. Grant me the endurance for the race and the joy of seeing it completed. Thank you Jesus for interceding for me, and as You have begun a good work in me, I cry, 'Complete it! Complete it!' Amen!

For further reading:

Philippians 1:6; 3:12-14; 2 Timothy 4:7-8

ENDORSEMENTS

In the years that I have known Kevin Sambrook I have found him to be an extraordinary gentlemen, a wordsmith and a man of deep biblical foundations with great prophetic hunger. Like myself, Kevin has a keen interest in history and the extraction of fundamental Kingdom principles that will help us in these last days. The Lord once told me some of the great champions of the past are prototypes of the army to emerge in the future. Certainly, Saint Patrick is one such example. In this book Kevin skillfully examines Patrick's life, his trials, victories and life experiences that forged the message he carried to his generation. Clearly, like John the Baptist, Patrick was a prophetic voice to the age in which he lived and exemplified a life lived in union with the Messiah. Without a doubt, this book will help prepare us for the days ahead and encourage us with the hope that leads to the Tree of Life.

Paul Keith Davis
WhiteDove Ministries

Because of my own Irish heritage I've long been fascinated by the life of St. Patrick. But biographies of this amazing Christian evangelist are often lacking in spiritual depth. That's why I am so grateful for the work of Kevin Sambrook, who has been studying St. Patrick's life, writings and ministry for many years. This book removes some of the mystery from the man and reveals his character, his faith and his compassion. You will learn that this hero of 4th century Ireland has much to say to us today.

J. Lee Grady
Former Editor, Charisma Magazine
Director, The Mordecai Project

46203083R00053

Made in the USA
San Bernardino, CA
28 February 2017